W9-BLG-027

892.78   Gibran

The secrets of the heart.
                                139862

Date Due

APR 29 1985	OCT 2 2 1992	
FEB 19 1988	OCT 2 6 2000	
MAR 1 4 1991		
APR 0 2 1992	MAY 3 1 2011	
JUN 0 4 1992		

MAYWOOD, ILL. PUBLIC LIBRARY
121 S. 5th Ave.
Phone 343-1847

Hours: Mon. & Thurs
            9:00 A.M.—9:00 P.M.
            Fri. & Sat. 9:00 A.M.—5:30 P.M.

BRANCH LIBRARY 840 S. 17th Ave.
Phone 343-0508

            Mon.—Fri.
            1:00 P.M.—5:30 P.M.
            Sat. 9:00 A.M.—5:30 P.M.

KAHLIL GIBRAN

the Secrets of the Heart

A Special Selection

THE WISDOM LIBRARY

A Division of

PHILOSOPHICAL LIBRARY

New York

© Copyright, 1971, by

Philosophical Library, Inc.

15 East 40th Street, New York, N. Y.

All rights reserved

SBN 8022-2080-0

TRANSLATED FROM THE ARABIC
BY ANTHONY RIZCALLAH FERRIS
and
EDITED BY MARTIN L. WOLF

Distributed to the Trade by
BOOK SALES, INC.
352 Park Avenue South
New York 10, N.Y. 10010

MANUFACTURED IN THE UNITED STATES OF AMERICA

Contents

139862

Editor's Preface

Although these atmospheric writings appear to be autobiographical in nature, they clearly reveal Kahlil Gibran as a prophet of penetrating vision and objective understanding. This seer warns ominously of the grave and unseen dangers yet to befall this world on its stony path of intrigue, maladjustment, and border consciousness. His clarity of perception is not confined to recognition and condemnation alone, but with a sincere constructive purpose motivated by his intense artist's faith in ultimate perfection, he offers strikingly logical methods for curing "the gaping wounds in the side of society." His warnings are neither crusades nor preachments, yet his thoughts are conveyed completely, clearly, powerfully. He muses over the beautiful, not the ugly, and his criticisms are heavily imbued with a gentle melancholy. All, however, are subordinated to his magnificent descriptive powers, abounding with fine metaphorical terseness.

On the ecclesiastical side, he displays a brilliance of spiritual insight and a determination of dedication that persist and probe until they pierce the outer self. His millions of followers in dozens of languages absorb Gibran's writings practically as religious devotions, and his excommunication served to fortify and augment his literary parish. His views of the church are more denunciatory than complimentary, but his love for its teachings and his fury over its methods are sharply defined, and bespeak no ambiguity or paradox in his meaning.

The book burners and clergy lived to rue their acts, and shortly before his death in 1931—perhaps when he was too weak to resist—Gibran submitted to the uninvited overtures of the church to reclaim him after the hasty excommunication. Despite the fact that "The Beloved Master" brought down the unconcealed wrath of religious and state authorities, any apology on his part was of little concern to him, for he had long since reached a spiritual plane far above petty rote, law, and doctrine.

MARTIN L. WOLF

The Secrets of the Heart

The Secrets of the Heart

A MAJESTIC MANSION stood under the wings of the silent night, as Life stands under the cover of Death. In it sat a maiden at an ivory desk, leaning her beautiful head on her soft hand, as a withering lily leans upon its petals. She looked around, feeling like a miserable prisoner, struggling to penetrate the walls of the dungeon with her eyes in order to witness Life walking in the procession of Freedom.

The hours passed like the ghosts of the night, as a procession chanting the dirge of her sorrow, and the maiden felt secure with the shedding of her tears in anguished solitude. When she could not resist the pressure of her suffering any longer, and as she felt that she was in full possession of the treasured secrets of her heart, she took the quill and commenced mingling her tears with ink upon parchment, and she inscribed:

"My Beloved Sister,

"When the heart becomes congested with secrets, and the eyes begin to burn from the searing tears, and the ribs are about to burst with the growing of the heart's confinement, one cannot find expression for such a labyrinth except by a surge of release.

"Sorrowful persons find joy in lamentation, and lovers encounter comfort and condolence in dreams, and the oppressed delight in receiving sympathy. I am writing to you now because I feel like a poet who fancies the beauty of objects whose impression he composes in verse while being ruled by a divine power. . . . I am like a child of the starving poor who cries for food, instigated by bitterness of hunger, disregarding the plight of his poor and merciful mother and her defeat in life.

"Listen to my painful story, my dear sister, and weep with me, for sobbing is like a prayer, and the tears of mercy are like a charity because they come forth from a living and sensitive and good soul and they are not shed in vain. It was the will of my father when I married a noble and rich man. My

4

father was like most of the rich, whose only joy in life is to improve their wealth by adding more gold to their coffers in fear of poverty, and curry nobility with grandeur in anticipation of the attacks of the black days. . . . I find myself now, with all my love and dreams, a victim upon a golden altar which I hate, and an inherited honour which I despise.

"I respect my husband because he is generous and kind to all; he endeavours to bring happiness to me, and spends his gold to please my heart, but I have found that the impression of all these things is not worth one moment of a true and divine love. Do not ridicule me, my sister, for I am now a most enlightened person regarding the needs of a woman's heart—that throbbing heart which is like a bird flying in the spacious sky of love. . . It is like a vase replenished with the wine of the ages that has been pressed for the sipping souls. . . . It is like a book in whose pages one reads the chapters of happiness and misery, joy and pain, laughter and sorrow. No one can read this book except the true companion who is the other half of the woman, created for her since the beginning of the world.

"Yes, I became most knowing amongst all women as to the purpose of the soul and meaning of the heart, for I have found that my magnificent horses and beautiful carriages and glittering coffers of gold and sublime nobility are not worth one glance from the eyes of that poor young man who is patiently waiting and suffering the pangs of bitterness and misery. . . . That youth who is oppressed by the cruelty and will of my father, and imprisoned in the narrow and melancholy jail of Life. . . .

"Please, my dear, do not contrive to console me, for the calamity through which I have realized the power of my love is my great consoler. Now I am looking forward from behind my tears and awaiting the coming of Death to lead me to where I will meet the companion of my soul and embrace him as I did before we entered this strange world.

"Do not think evil of me, for I am doing my duty as a faithful wife, and complying calmly and patiently with the laws and rules of man. I honour my husband with my sense, and respect him with my heart, and revere him with my soul, but there is a withholding, for God gave part of me to my beloved before I knew him.

"Heaven willed that I spend my life with a man not meant for me, and I am wasting my days silently according to the will of Heaven; but if the gates of Eternity do not open, I will remain with the beautiful half of my soul and look back to the Past, and that Past is this Present. . . . I shall look at life as Spring looks at Winter, and contemplate the obstacles of Life as one who has climbed the rough trail and reached the mountain top."

*   *   *   *   *

At that moment the maiden ceased writing and hid her face with her cupped hands and wept bitterly. Her heart declined to entrust to the pen its most sacred secrets, but resorted to the pouring of dry tears that dispersed quickly and mingled with the gentle ether, the haven of the lovers' souls and the flowers' spirits. After a moment she took the quill and added, "Do you remember that youth? Do you recollect the rays which emanated from his eyes, and the sorrowful signs upon his face? Do you recall that laughter which bespoke the tears of a mother, torn from her only child? Can you retrace his serene voice speaking the echo of a distant valley? Do you remember him meditating and staring longingly and calmly at objects and speaking of them in strange words, and then bending his head and sighing as if fearing to reveal the secrets of his great heart? Do you recall his dreams and beliefs? Do you recollect all these things in a youth whom humanity counts as one of her children and upon whom my father looked with eyes of superiority because he is higher than earthly greed and nobler than inherited grandeur?

"You know, my dear sister, that I am a martyr in this belittling world, and a victim of ignorance. Will you sympathize with a sister who sits in the silence of the horrible night pouring down the contents of her inner self and revealing to you her heart's secrets? I am sure that you will sympathize

8

with me, for I know that Love has visited your heart."

*   *   *   *   *

Dawn came, and the maiden surrendered herself to Slumber, hoping to find sweeter and more gentle dreams than those she had encountered in her awakeness. . . .

My Countrymen

My Countrymen

WHAT DO YOU SEEK, My Countrymen?
Do you desire that I build for
You gorgeous palaces, decorated
With words of empty meaning, or
Temples roofed with dreams? Or
Do you command me to destroy what
The liars and tyrants have built?
Shall I uproot with my fingers
What the hypocrites and the wicked
Have implanted? Speak your insane
Wish!

What is it you would have me do,
My Countrymen? Shall I purr like
The kitten to satisfy you, or roar
Like the lion to please myself? I
Have sung for you, but you did not
Dance; I have wept before you, but

You did not cry. Shall I sing and
Weep at the same time?

Your souls are suffering the pangs
Of hunger, and yet the fruit of
Knowledge is more plentiful than
The stones of the valleys.

Your hearts are withering from
Thirst, and yet the springs of
Life are streaming about your
Homes—why do you not drink?
The sea has its ebb and flow,
The moon has its fullness and
Crescents, and the Ages have
Their winter and summer, and all
Things vary like the shadow of
An unborn God moving between
Earth and sun, but Truth cannot
Be changed, nor will it pass away;
Why, then, do you endeavour to
Disfigure its countenance?

I have called you in the silence
Of the night to point out the
Glory of the moon and the dignity
Of the stars, but you startled
From your slumber and clutched
Your swords in fear, crying,
"Where is the enemy? We must kill
Him first!" At morningtide, when
The enemy came, I called to you
Again, but now you did not wake
From your slumber, for you were
Locked in fear, wrestling with
The processions of spectres in
Your dreams.

And I said unto you, "Let us climb
To the mountain top and view the
Beauty of the world." And you
Answered me, saying, "In the depths
Of this valley our fathers lived,
And in its shadow they died, and in
Its caves they were buried. How can

We depart this place for one which
They failed to honour?"

And I said unto you, "Let us go to
The plain that gives its bounty to
The sea." And you spoke timidly to
Me, saying, "The uproar of the abyss
Will frighten our spirits, and the
Terror of the depths will deaden
Our bodies."

       *   *   *   *   *

I have loved you, My Countrymen, but
My love for you is painful to me
And useless to you; and today I
Hate you, and hatred is a flood
That sweeps away the dry branches
And quavering houses.

I have pitied your weakness, My
Countrymen, but my pity has but
Increased your feebleness, exalting
And nourishing slothfulness which

Is vain to Life. And today I see
Your infirmity which my soul loathes
And fears.

I have cried over your humiliation
And submission; and my tears streamed
Like crystalline, but could not sear
Away your stagnant weakness; yet they
Removed the veil from my eyes.

My tears have never reached your
Petrified hearts, but they cleansed
The darkness from my inner self.
Today I am mocking at your suffering,
For laughter is a raging thunder that
Precedes the tempest and never comes
After it.

What do you desire, My Countrymen?
Do you wish for me to show you
The ghost of your countenance on
The face of still water? Come,
Now, and see how ugly you are!

Look and meditate! Fear has
Turned your hair grey as the
Ashes, and dissipation has grown
Over your eyes and made them into
Obscured hollows, and cowardice
Has touched your cheeks that now
Appear as dismal pits in the
Valley, and Death has kissed
Your lips and left them yellow
As the Autumn leaves.

What is it that you seek, My
Countrymen? What ask you from
Life, who does not any longer
Count you among her children?

Your souls are freezing in the
Clutches of the priests and
Sorcerers, and your bodies
Tremble between the paws of the
Despots and the shedders of
Blood, and your country quakes
Under the marching feet of the

Conquering enemy; what may you
Expect even though you stand
Proudly before the face of the
Sun? Your swords are sheathed
With rust, and your spears are
Broken, and your shields are
Laden with gaps; why, then, do
You stand in the field of battle?

Hypocrisy is your religion, and
Falsehood is your life, and
Nothingness is your ending; why,
Then, are you living? Is not
Death the sole comfort of the
Miserables?

*   *   *   *   *

Life is a resolution that
Accompanies youth, and a diligence
That follows maturity, and a
Wisdom that pursues senility; but
You, My Countrymen, were born old
And weak. And your skins withered

And your heads shrank, whereupon
You became as children, running
Into the mire and casting stones
Upon each other.

Knowledge is a light, enriching
The warmth of life, and all may
Partake who seek it out; but you,
My Countrymen, seek out darkness
And flee the light, awaiting the
Coming of water from the rock,
And your nation's misery is your
Crime. . . . I do not forgive you
Your sins, for you know what you
Are doing.

Humanity is a brilliant river
Singing its way and carrying with
It the mountains' secrets into
The heart of the sea; but you,
My Countrymen, are stagnant
Marshes infested with insects
And vipers.

The Spirit is a sacred blue
Torch, burning and devouring
The dry plants, and growing
With the storm and illuminating
The faces of the goddesses; but
You, My Countrymen . . . your souls
Are like ashes which the winds
Scatter upon the snow, and which
The tempests disperse forever in
The valleys.

Fear not the phantom of Death,
My Countrymen, for his greatness
And mercy will refuse to approach
Your smallness; and dread not the
Dagger, for it will decline to be
Lodged in your shallow hearts.

I hate you, My Countrymen, because
You hate glory and greatness. I
Despise you because you despise
Yourselves. I am your enemy, for
You refuse to realize that you are
The enemies of the goddesses.

John the Madman

John the Madman

IN SUMMER John walked every morning into the field, driving his oxen and carrying his plough over his shoulder, hearkening to the soothing songs of the birds and the rustling of the leaves and the grass.

At noon he sat beside a brook in the colourful prairies for repast, leaving a few morsels upon the green grass for the birds of the sky.

At eventide he returned to his wretched hovel that stood apart from those hamlets and villages in North Lebanon. After the evening meal he sat and listened attentively to his parents, who related tales of the past ages until sleep allured and captured his eyes.

In winter he spent his days by the fireside, pondering the wailing of the winds and lamentation of the elements, meditating upon the phenomena of the seasons, and looking through the window toward the snow-laden valleys and leafless trees, symbolizing a multitude of suffering people left helpless in the jaws of biting frost and strong wind.

During the long winter nights he sat up until his parents retired, whereupon he opened a rough wooden closet, brought out his New Testament, and read it secretly under the dim light of a flickering lamp. The priests objected to the reading of the Good Book, and John exercised great caution during these fascinating moments of study. The fathers warned the simple-hearted people against its use, and threatened them with excommunication from the church if discovered possessing it.

Thus John spent his youth between the beautiful earth of God and the New Testament, full of light and truth. John was a youth of silence and contemplation; he listened to his parents' conversations and never spoke a word nor asked a question. When sitting with his contemporaries, he gazed steadily at the horizon, and his thoughts were as distant as his eyes. After each visit to the church he returned home with a depressed spirit, for the teachings of the priests were different from the precepts he found in the Gospel, and the life of the faithful was not the beautiful life of which Christ spoke.

*   *   *   *   *

Spring came and the snow melted in the fields and valleys. The snow upon the mountain tops was thawing gradually and forming many stream-lets in the winding paths leading into the valleys, combining into a torrent whose roaring bespoke the awakening of Nature. The almond and apple trees were in full bloom; the willow and poplar trees were sprouting with buds, and Nature had spread her happy and colourful garments over the countryside.

John, tired of spending his days by the fireside, and knowing that his oxen were longing for the pastures, released his animals from the sheds and led them to the fields, concealing his New Testa-ment under his cloak for fear of detection. He reached a beautiful arbor adjacent to some fields belonging to the St. Elija Monastery * which stood majestically upon a nearby hill. As the oxen commenced grazing, John leaned upon a rock and began to read his New Testament and meditate the sadness of the children of God on earth, and the beauty of the Kingdom of Heaven.

It was the last day of Lent, and the villagers who abstained from eating meat were impatiently awaiting the coming of Easter. John, like the rest of the poor fellahin, never distinguished Lent from any other day of the year, for his whole life was an extended Lent, and his food never exceeded the simple bread, kneaded with the pain of his heart, or the fruits, purchased with the blood of his body. The only nourishment craved by John during Lent was that spiritual food—the heavenly bread that brought into his heart sad thoughts of the tragedy of the Son of Man and the end of His life on earth.

The birds were singing and hovering about him, and large flocks of doves circled in the sky,

---

* A rich abbey in North Lebanon with vast lands, occupied by scores of monks called Alepoans. (Editor's note.)

while the flowers swayed with the breeze as if exhilarated by the brilliant sunshine.

John busied himself absorbing the Book, and between these intense, light-giving sessions, he watched the domes of the churches in the nearby villages and listened to the rhythmic toll of the bells. Occasionally he would close his eyes and fly on the wings of dreams to Old Jerusalem, following Christ's steps and asking the people of the city about the Nazarene, whereupon he would receive the answer, "Here He cured the paralyzed and restored to the blind their sight; and there they braided for Him a wreath of thorns and placed it upon His head; from that portico He spoke to the multitude with beautiful parables; in that palace they tied Him to the marble columns and scourged Him; on this road He forgave the adulteress her sins, and upon that spot He fell under the weight of His Cross."

.*   *   *   *   *

One hour passed, and John was suffering physically with God and glorifying with Him in spirit.

Noon quickly came, and the oxen were beyond the reach of John's sight. He looked in every direction but could not see them, and as he reached the trail that led to the adjacent fields, he saw a man at a distance, standing amidst the orchards. As he approached and saw that the man was one of the Monastery's monks, he greeted him, bowed reverently, and asked him if he had seen the oxen. The monk appeared to be restraining anger, and he said, "Yes, I saw them. Follow me and I will show them to you." As they reached the Monastery, John found his oxen tied with ropes in a shed. One of the monks was acting as a watchman over them, and each time an animal moved, he struck the ox across the back with a heavy club. John made a frantic attempt to unbind the helpless animals, but the monk took hold of his cloak and withheld him. At the same time he turned toward the Monastery and shouted, saying, "Here is the criminal shepherd! I have found him!" The priests and monks, preceded by the head priest, hurried to the scene and encircled John, who was bewildered, and felt like a captive. "I have done nothing to merit the treatment of a criminal," said John to the head priest. And the leader replied angrily, "Your oxen have ruined our plantation and destroyed our vineyards. Since you are responsible for the damage we will not give up your oxen until you adjust our loss."

John protested, "I am poor and have no money. Please release my oxen and I pledge my honour that I will never again bring them to these lands." The head priest took a step forward, raised his hand toward heaven, and said, "God has appointed us to be the protectors over this vast land of St. Elija, and it is our sacred duty to guard it with all of our might, for this land is holy, and, like fire, it will burn any who trespass upon it. If you refuse to account for your crime against God, the grass that your oxen have eaten will surely turn into poison and destroy them!"

The head priest started to depart, but John touched his robe and humbly begged, "I appeal to you in the name of Jesus and all the saints, to let me and my animals free. Be kind to me, for I am poor, and the coffers of the Monastery are bursting with silver and gold. Have mercy upon my poor and aged parents, whose lives depend on me. God will forgive me if I have harmed you." The head priest looked at him with severity, and said, "Poor or rich, the Monastery cannot forgive you your debts; three denars will free your oxen." John pleaded, "I do not possess a single coin; have mercy on a poor grazier, Father." And the head priest retorted, "Then you must sell a part of your possessions and bring three denars, for it is better to enter the Kingdom of Heaven without property than to bring the wrath of St. Elija upon you and descend to hell." The other monks nodded their accord.

After a short silence, John's face brightened and his eyes shone as if fear and servility had deserted his heart. With his head high, he looked at the head priest and addressed him boldly, saying, "Do the weak poor have to sell their pitiful belongings, the source of their life's bread, in order to add more gold to the Monastery's wealth? Is it just that the poor should be oppressed and made poorer in order that St. Elija may forgive

32

the oxen their innocent wrongs?" The head priest raised his eyes to heaven and intoned, "It is written in the Book of God that he who has plenty shall be given more, and he who has not shall be taken from."

When John heard these words he became furious, and like a soldier who draws his sword in the face of the enemy, he drew the New Testament from his pocket and shouted out, "This is how you twist the teachings of Christ, you hypocrite! And thus do you pervert the most sacred heritage of life in order to spread your evils. . . . Woe to you when the Son of Man comes again and destroys your Monastery and throws its debris in the valley, and burns your shrine and altars into ashes. . . . Woe to you when the wrath of the Nazarene descends upon you and throws you into the depths of the abyss. . . . Woe to you, worshippers of the idols of greed, who hide the ugliness of hatred under your black garments. . . . Woe to you, foes of Jesus, who move your lips with prayers while your hearts are laden with lusts. . . . Woe to you who kneel before the altar in body while your spirits are revolting against God! You are polluted with your own sin of punishing me for approaching your land, paid for by me and my ancestors. You ridiculed me when I asked for mercy in the name of Christ. Take this Book and show your smiling monks where the Son of God ever refused to forgive. . . . Read this heavenly tragedy and tell them where He spoke not of mercy and of kindness, be it in the Sermon of the Mount, or in the temple. Did He not forgive the adulteress her sins? Did He not part his hands upon the Cross to embrace humanity? Look upon our wretched homes, where the sick suffer upon their hard beds. . . . Look behind the prison bars, where the innocent man is victim of oppression and injustice. . . . Look upon the beggars, stretching forth their hands for alms, humiliated in heart and broken in body. . . . Think upon your slaving followers, who are suffering the pangs of hunger while you are living a life of luxury and indifference, and enjoying the fruits of the fields and the wine of the vineyards. You have never visited a sufferer nor consoled the down-hearted nor fed the hungry; neither have you sheltered the wayfarer nor offered sympathy to the lame. Yet you are not satisfied with what you have pilfered from our fathers, but still stretch your hands like vipers' heads, grasping by threats of hell what little a widow has saved through body-breaking toil, or a miserable fellah has stored away to keep his children alive!"

John took a deep breath, then calmed his voice and quietly added, "You are numerous, and I am alone—you may do unto me what you wish; the wolves prey upon the lamb in the darkness of the night, but the blood stains remain upon the stones in the valley until the dawn comes, and the sun reveals the crime to all."

There was a magic power in John's talk that arrested their attention and injected a defensive anger into the monks' hearts. They were shaking with fury and waiting only for their superior's order to fall upon John and bring him to submission. The brief silence was like the heavy quiet of the tempest, after laying waste the gardens. The head priest then commanded the monks, saying, "Bind this criminal and take the Book from him and drag him into a dark cell, for he who blasphemes the holy representatives of God will never be forgiven on this earth, neither in Eternity." The Monks leaped upon John and led him manacled into a narrow prison and barred him there.

The courage shown by John could not be perceived or understood by one who partakes of the submission or the deceit or the tyranny of this enslaved country, called by the Orientals "The Bride of Syria," and "The Pearl of the Sultan's Crown." And in his cell, John thought of the needless misery brought upon his countrymen by the grip of the things he had just learned. He smiled with a sad sympathy and his smile was mingled with suffering and bitterness; the kind that cuts its way through the depths of the heart; the kind that sets the soul to a choking futility; the kind which, if left unsupported, ascends to the eyes and falls down helplessly.

John then stood proudly, and looked through the window-slit facing the sunlit valley. He felt as if a spiritual joy were embracing his soul and a sweet tranquility possessing his heart. They had imprisoned his body, but his spirit was sailing freely with the breeze amidst the knolls and prairies. His love for Jesus never changed, and the torturing hands could not remove his heart's ease, for persecution cannot harm him who stands by Truth. Did not Socrates fall proudly a victim in body? Was not Paul stoned for the sake of the Truth? It is our inner selves that hurt us when we disobey it, and it kills us when we betray it.

* * * * *

John's parents were informed of his imprisonment and the confiscation of the oxen. His old mother came to the Monastery leaning heavily over her walking stick and she prostrated herself before the head priest, kissing his feet and begging him for mercy upon her only son. The head priest raised his head reverently toward heaven and said, "We will forgive your son for his madness, but St. Elija will not forgive any who trespass upon his land." After gazing at him with

37

tearful eyes, the old lady took a silver locket from her neck and handed it to the head priest, saying, "This is my most precious possession, given to me as a wedding gift by my mother. . . . Will you accept it as atonement for my son's sin?"

The head priest took the locket and placed it in his pocket, whereupon he looked at John's ancient mother who was kissing his hands and expressing to him her thanks and gratitude, and he said, "Woe to this sinful age! You twist the saying of the Good Book and cause the children to eat the sour, and the parents' teeth sit on edge; go now, good woman, and pray to God for your mad son and ask Him to restore his mind."

John left the prison, and walked quietly by the side of his mother, driving the oxen before him. When they reached their wretched hovel, he led the animals into their mangers and sat silently by the window, meditating the sunset. In a few moments he heard his father whispering to his mother, saying, "Sara, many times have I told you that John was mad, and you disbelieved. Now you will agree, after what you have seen, for the head priest has spoken to you today the very words I spoke to you in past years." John continued looking toward the distant horizon, watching the sun descend.

*   *   *   *   *

Easter arrived, and at that time the construction of a new church in the town of Bsherri had just been completed. This magnificent place of worship was like a prince's palace standing amidst the huts of poor subjects. The people were scurrying through the many preparations to receive a prelate who was assigned to officiate at the religious ceremonies inaugurating the new temple. The multitudes stood in rows over the roads waiting for His Grace's arrival. The chanting of the priests in unison with cymbal sounds and the hymns of the throngs filled the sky.

The prelate finally arrived, riding a magnificent horse harnessed with a gold-studded saddle, and as he dismounted, the priests and political leaders met him with the most beautiful of welcoming speeches. He was escorted to the new altar, where he clothed himself in ecclesiastical raiment, decorated with gold threads and encrusted with sparkling gems; he wore the golden crown, and walked in a procession around the altar, carrying his jewelled staff. He was followed by the priests and the carriers of tapers and incense burners.

At that hour, John stood amongst the fellahin at the portico, contemplating the scene with bitter sighs and sorrowful eyes, for it pained him to observe the expensive robes, and precious crown, and staff, and vases and other objects of needless extravagance, while the poor fellahin who came from the surrounding villages to celebrate the occasion were suffering the gnawing pangs of poverty. Their tattered swaddles and sorrowful faces bespoke their miserable plight.

The rich dignitaries, decorated with badges and ribbons, stood aloof praying loudly, while the suffering villagers, in the rear of the scene, beat their bosoms in sincere prayer that came from the depths of their broken hearts.

The authority of those dignitaries and leaders

40

was like the ever-green leaves of the poplar trees, and the life of those fellahin was like a boat whose pilot had met his destiny and whose rudder had been lost and whose sails had been torn by the strong wind and left at the mercy of the furious depths and the raging tempest.

Tyranny and blind submission . . . which one of these gave birth to the other? Is tyranny a strong tree that grows not in the low earth, or is it submission, which is like a deserted field where naught but thorns can grow? Such thoughts and contemplations prayed on John's mind while the ceremonies were taking place; he braced his arms about his chest for fear his bosom would burst with agony over the people's plight in this tragedy of opposites.

He gazed upon the withering creatures of severe humanity, whose hearts were dry and whose seeds were now seeking shelter in the bosom of the earth, as destitute pilgrims seek rebirth in a new realm.

When the pageantry came to an end and the multitude was preparing to disperse, John felt that a compelling power was urging him to speak in behalf of the oppressed poor. He proceeded to an extreme end of the square, raised his hands toward the sky, and as the throngs gathered about, he opened his lips and said, "O Jesus, Who art sitting in the heart of the circle of light, give heed! Look upon this earth from behind the blue dome and see how the thorns have choked the flowers which Thy truth hast planted.

"Oh Good Shepherd, the wolves have preyed upon the weak lamb which Thou hast carried in Thy arms. Thy pure blood has been drawn into the depths of the earth which Thy feet have made sacred. This good earth has been made by Thine enemies into an arena where the strong crushes the weak. The cry of the miserable and the lamentation of the helpless can no longer be heard by those sitting upon the thrones, preaching Thy word. The lambs which Thou hast sent to this earth are now wolves who eat the one which Thou hast carried and blessed.

"The word of light which sprang forth from Thy heart has vanished from the scripture and is replaced with an empty and terrible uproar that frightens the spirit.

"Oh Jesus, they have built these churches for the sake of their own glory, and embellished them with silk and melted gold. . . . They left the bodies of Thy chosen poor wrapped in tattered raiment in the cold night. . . . They filled the sky with the smoke of burning candles and incense and left the bodies of Thy faithful worshippers empty of bread. . . . They raised their voices with hymns of praise, but deafened themselves to the cry and moan of the widows and orphans.

"Come again, Oh Living Jesus, and drive the vendors of Thy faith from Thy sacred temple, for they have turned it into a dark cave where vipers of hypocrisy and falsehood crawl and abound."

John's words, strong and sincere, brought murmurs of approval, and the approach of the dignitaries quelled him not. With added courage, strengthened by memories of his earlier experience, he continued, "Come, Oh Jesus, and render accounts with those Caesars who usurped from the weak what is the weak's and from God what is God's. The grapevine which Thou has planted with Thy right hand has been eaten by worms of greed and its bunches have been trampled down. Thy sons of peace are dividing amongst themselves and fighting one with another, leaving poor souls as victims in the wintry field. Before Thy altar, they raise their voices with prayers, saying, 'Glory to God in the highest, and on earth peace, good will toward men.' Will our Father in heaven be glorified when His name is uttered by empty hearts and sinful lips and false tongues? Will peace be on earth while the sons of misery are slaving in the fields to feed the strong and fill the stomachs of the tyrants? Will ever peace come and save them from the clutches of destitution?

"What is peace? Is it in the eyes of those infants, nursing upon the dry breasts of their hungry mothers in cold huts? Or is it in the wretched hovels of the hungry who sleep upon hard beds and crave for one bite of the food which the priests and monks feed to their fat pigs?

"What is joy, Oh Beautiful Jesus? Is it manifest

when the Emir buys the strong arms of men and the honour of women for threats of death or for a few pieces of silver? Or is it found in submission, and slaving of body and spirit to those who dazzle our eyes with their glittering badges and golden diadems? Upon each complaint to Thy peace makers, they reward us with their soldiers, armed with swords and spears to step upon our women and children and steal our blood.

"Oh Jesus, full of love and mercy, stretch forth Thy strong arms and protect us from those thieves or send welcome Death to deliver us and lead us to the graves where we can rest peacefully under the watchful care of Thy Cross; there we shall wait for Thy return. Oh Mighty Jesus, this life is naught but a dark cell of enslavement. . . . It is a playing ground of horrible ghosts, and it is a pit alive with spectres of death. Our days are but sharp swords concealed under the ragged quilts of our beds in the fearful darkness of the night. At dawn, these weapons rise above our heads as demons, pointing out to us our whip-driven slavery in the fields.

"Oh Jesus, have mercy upon the oppressed poor who came today to commemorate Thy Resurrection. . . . Pity them, for they are miserable and weak."

John's talk appealed to one group and displeased another. "He is telling the truth, and speaking in our behalf before heaven," one remarked. And another one said, "He is bewitched, for he speaks in the name of an evil spirit." And a third commented, "We have never heard such infamous talk, not even from our fathers! We must bring it to an end!" And a fourth one said, whispering into the next man's ears, "I felt a new spirit in me when I heard him talking." The next man added, "But the priests know our needs more so than he does; it is a sin to doubt them." As the voices grew from every direction like the roar of the sea, one of the priests approached, placed John in restraint and turned him immediately to the law, whereupon he was taken to the Governor's palace for trial.

Upon his interrogation, John uttered not a single word, for he knew that the Nazarene resorted to silence before His persecutors. The governor ordered John to be placed in a prison, where he slept peacefully and heart-cleansed that night, leaning his head on the rock wall of the dungeon.

The next day John's father came and testified before the Governor that his son was mad, and added, sadly, "Many times have I heard him talking to himself and speaking of many strange things that none could see or understand. Many times did he sit talking in the silence of the night, using vague words. I heard him calling the ghosts with a voice like that of a sorcerer. You may ask the neighbours who talked to him and found beyond doubt that he was insane. He never answered when one spoke to him, and when he spoke, he uttered cryptic words and phrases unknown to the listener and out of the subject. His mother knows him well. Many times she saw him gazing at the distant horizon with glazed eyes and speaking with passion, like a small child, about the brooks and the flowers and the stars. Ask the monks whose teachings he ridiculed and criticized during their sacred Lent. He is insane,

Your Excellency, but he is very kind to me and to his mother; he does much to help us in our old age, and he works with diligence to keep us fed and warm and alive. Pity him, and have mercy on us."

The Governor released John, and the news of his madness spread throughout the village. And when the people spoke of John they mentioned his name with humour and ridicule, and the maidens looked upon him with sorrowful eyes and said, "Heaven has its strange purpose in man. . . . God united beauty and insanity in this youth, and joined the kind brightness of his eyes with the darkness of his unseen self."

*　　*　　*　　*　　*

In the midst of God's fields and prairies, and by the side of the knolls, carpeted with green grass and beautiful flowers, the ghost of John, alone and restless, watches the oxen grazing peacefully, undisturbed by man's hardships. With tearful eyes he looks toward the scattered villages on both sides of the valley and repeats with deep sighs, "You are numerous and I am alone; the wolves prey upon the lambs in the darkness of the night, but the blood stains remain upon the stones in the valley until the dawn comes, and the sun reveals the crime to all."

The Enchanting Houri

The Enchanting Houri

WHERE are you leading me, Oh Enchanting
Houri, and how long shall I follow you
Upon this hispid road, planted with
Thorns? How long shall our souls ascend
And descend painfully on this twisting
And rocky path?

Like a child following his mother I am
Following you, holding the extreme end
Of your garment, forgetting my dreams
And staring at your beauty, blinding
My eyes under your spell to the
Procession of spectres hovering above
Me, and attracted to you by an inner
Force within me which I cannot deny.

Halt for a moment and let me see your
Countenance; and look upon me for a

Moment; perhaps I will learn your
Heart's secrets through your strange
Eyes. Stop and rest, for I am weary,
And my soul is trembling with fear
Upon this horrible trail. Halt, for
We have reached that terrible crossroad
Where Death embraces Life.

*　　*　　*　　*　　*

Oh Houri, listen to me! I was as free
As the birds, probing the valleys and
The forests, and flying in the spacious
Sky. At eventide I rested upon the
Branches of the trees, meditating the
Temples and palaces in the City of the
Colorful Clouds which the Sun builds
In the morning and destroys before
Twilight.

I was like a thought, walking alone
And at peace to the East and West of
The Universe, rejoicing with the
Beauty and joy of Life, and inquiring

Into the magnificent mystery of
Existence.

I was like a dream, stealing out under
The friendly wings of the night,
Entering through the closed windows
Into the maidens' chambers, frolicking
And awakening their hopes. . . . Then I
Sat by the youths and agitated their
Desires. . . . Then I probed the elders'
Quarters and penetrated their thoughts
Of serene contentment.

Then you captured my fancy, and since
That hypnotic moment I felt like a
Prisoner dragging his shackles and
Impelled into an unknown place. . . .
I became intoxicated with your sweet
Wine that has stolen my will, and I
Now find my lips kissing the hand
That strikes me sharply. Can you
Not see with your soul's eye the
Crushing of my heart? Halt for a

Moment; I am regaining my strength
And untying my weary feet from the
Heavy chains. I have crushed the
Cup from which I have drunk your
Tasty venom. . . . But now I am in
A strange land, and bewildered;
Which road shall I follow?

My freedom has been restored; will
You now accept me as a willing
Companion, who looks at the Sun
With glazed eyes and grasps the
Fire with untrembling fingers?

I have unbound my wings and I am
Ready to ascend; will you accompany
A youth who spends his days roaming
The mountains like the lone eagle, and
Wastes his nights wandering in the
Deserts like the restless lion?

Will you content yourself with the
Affection of one who looks upon Love

As but an entertainer, and declines
To accept her as his master?

Will you accept a heart that loves,
But never yields? And burns, but
Never melts? Will you be at ease
With a soul that quivers before the
Tempest, but never surrenders to it?
Will you accept one as a companion
Who makes not slaves, nor will become
One? Will you own me but not possess
Me, by taking my body and not my heart?

Then here is my hand—grasp it with
Your beautiful hand; and here is my
Body—embrace it with your loving
Arms; and here are my lips—bestow
Upon them a deep and dizzying kiss.

Behind the Garment

Behind the Garment

R<small>ACHEL</small> woke at midnight and gazed intently at something invisible in the sky of her chamber. She heard a voice more soothing than the whispers of Life, and more dismal than the moaning call of the abyss, and softer than the rustling of white wings, and deeper than the message of the waves. . . . It vibrated with hope and with futility, with joy and with misery, and with affection for life, yet with desire for death. Then Rachel closed her eyes and sighed deeply, and gasped, saying, "Dawn has reached the extreme end of the valley; we should go toward the sun and meet him." Her lips were parted, resembling and echoing a deep wound in the soul.

At that moment the priest approached her bed and felt her hand, but found it as cold as the snow; and when he grimly placed his fingers upon her heart, he determined that it was as immobile as the ages, and as silent as the secret of his heart.

The reverend father bowed his head in deep despair. His lips quivered as if wanting to utter a divine word, repeated by the phantoms of the night in the distant and deserted valleys.

After crossing her arms upon her bosom, the priest looked toward a man sitting in an obscured corner of the room, and with a kind and merciful voice he said, "Your beloved has reached the great circle of light. Come, my brother, let us kneel and pray."

The sorrowful husband lifted his head; his eyes stared, gazing at the unseen, and his expression then changed as if he saw understanding in the ghost of an unknown God. He gathered the remnants of himself and walked reverently toward the bed of his wife, and knelt by the side of the clergyman who was praying and lamenting and making the sign of the cross.

Placing his hand upon the shoulder of the grief-stricken husband, the Father said quietly, "Go to the adjoining room, brother, for you are in great need of rest."

He rose obediently, walked to the room and threw his fatigued body upon a narrow bed, and in a few moments he was sailing in the world of sleep like a little child taking refuge in the merciful arms of his loving mother.

*   *   *   *   *

The priest remained standing like a statue in the center of the room, and a strange conflict gripped him. And he looked with tearful eyes first at the cold body of the young woman and then through the parted curtain at her husband, who had surrendered himself to the allure of slumber. An hour, longer than an age and more terrible than Death, had already passed, and the priest was still standing between two parted souls. One was dreaming as a field dreams of the coming Spring after the tragedy of Winter, and the other was resting eternally.

Then the priest came close to the body of the young woman and knelt as if worshipping before

63

the altar; he held her cold hand and placed it against his trembling lips, and looked at her face that was adorned with the soft veil of Death. His voice was at the same time calm as the night and deep as the chasm and faltering as with the hopes of man. And in voice he wept, "Oh Rachel, bride of my soul, hear me! At last I am able to talk! Death has opened my lips so that I can now reveal to you a secret deeper than Life itself. Pain has unpinioned my tongue and I can disclose to you my suffering, more painful than pain. Listen to the cry of my soul, Oh Pure Spirit, hovering between the earth and the firmament. Give heed to the youth who waited for you to come from the field, gazing upon you from behind the trees, in fear of your beauty. Hear the priest, who is serving God, calling to you unashamed, after you have reached the City of God. I have proved the strength of my love by concealing it!"

Having thus opened his soul, the Father leaned over and printed three long, warm, and mute kisses upon her forehead, eyes and throat, pouring forth all his heart's secret of love and pain, and the anguish of the years. Then he suddenly withdrew to the dark corner and dropped in agony upon the floor, shaking like an Autumn leaf, as if the touch of her cold face had awakened within him the spirit to repent; whereupon he composed himself and knelt, hiding has face with his cupped hands, and he whispered softly, "God. . . . Forgive my sin; forgive my weakness, Oh Lord. I could no longer resist disclosing tnat which You knew. Seven years have I kept the deep secrets hidden in my heart from the spoken word, until Death came and tore them from me. Help me, Oh God, to hide this terrible and beautiful memory which brings sweetness from life and bitterness from You. Forgive me, My Lord, and forgive my weakness."

Without looking at the young woman's corpse, he continued suffering and lamenting until Dawn came and dropped a rosy veil upon those two still images, revealing the conflict of Love and Religion to one man; the peace of Life and Death to the other.

Dead Are My People

Dead Are My People

(Written in exile during the famine in Syria)
"WORLD WAR I"

Gone are my people, but I exist yet,
Lamenting them in my solitude. . . .
Dead are my friends, and in their
Death my life is naught but great
Disaster.

The knolls of my country are submerged
By tears and blood, for my people and
My beloved are gone, and I am here
Living as I did when my people and my
Beloved were enjoying life and the
Bounty of life, and when the hills of
My country were blessed and engulfed
By the light of the sun.

My people died from hunger, and he who
Did not perish from starvation was

69

Butchered with the sword; and I am
Here in this distant land, roaming
Amongst a joyful people who sleep
Upon soft beds, and smile at the days
While the days smile upon them.

My people died a painful and shameful
Death, and here am I living in plenty
And in peace. . . . This is deep tragedy
Ever-enacted upon the stage of my
Heart; few would care to witness this
Drama, for my people are as birds with
Broken wings, left behind by the flock.

If I were hungry and living amid my
Famished people, and persecuted among
My oppressed countrymen, the burden
Of the black days would be lighter
Upon my restless dreams, and the
Obscurity of the night would be less
Dark before my hollow eyes and my
Crying heart and my wounded soul.
For he who shares with his people

Their sorrow and agony will feel a
Supreme comfort created only by
Suffering in sacrifice. And he will
Be at peace with himself when he dies
Innocent with his fellow innocents.

But I am not living with my hungry
And persecuted people who are walking
In the procession of death toward
Martyrdom. . . . I am here beyond the
Broad seas living in the shadow of
Tranquility, and in the sunshine of
Peace. . . . I am afar from the pitiful
Arena and the distressed, and cannot
Be proud of aught, not even of my own
Tears.

What can an exiled son do for his
Starving people, and of what value
Unto them is the lamentation of an
Absent poet?

Were I an ear of corn grown in the earth
Of my country, the hungry child would

Pluck me and remove with my kernels
The hand of Death from his soul. Were
I a ripe fruit in the gardens of my
Country, the starving woman would
Gather me and sustain life. Were I
A bird flying in the sky of my country,
My hungry brother would hunt me and
Remove with the flesh of my body the
Shadow of the grave from his body.
But alas! I am not an ear of corn
Grown in the plains of Syria, nor a
Ripe fruit in the valleys of Lebanon;
This is my disaster, and this is my
Mute calamity which brings humiliation
Before my soul and before the phantoms
Of the night. . . .This is the painful
Tragedy which tightens my tongue and
Pinions my arms and arrests me usurped
Of power and of will and of action.
This is the curse burned upon my
Forehead before God and man.

*   *   *   *   *

And oftentime they say unto me,
"The disaster of your country is
But naught to the calamity of the
World, and the tears and blood shed
By your people are as nothing to
The rivers of blood and tears
Pouring each day and night in the
Valleys and plains of the earth. . . ."

Yes, but the death of my people is
A silent accusation; it is a crime
Conceived by the heads of the unseen
Serpents. . . . It is a songless and
Sceneless tragedy. . . . And if my
People had attacked the despots
And oppressors and died as rebels,
I would have said, "Dying for
Freedom is nobler than living in
The shadow of weak submission, for
He who embraces death with the sword
Of Truth in his hand will eternalize
With the Eternity of Truth, for Life

Is weaker than Death and Death is
Weaker than Truth.

If my nation had partaken in the war
Of all nations and had died in the
Field of battle, I would say that
The raging tempest had broken with
Its might the green branches; and
Strong death under the canopy of
The tempest is nobler than slow
Perishment in the arms of senility.
But there was no rescue from the
Closing jaws. . . . My people dropped
And wept with the crying angels.

If an earthquake had torn my
Country asunder and the earth had
Engulfed my people into its bosom,
I would have said, "A great and
Mysterious law has been moved by
The will of divine force, and it
Would be pure madness if we frail
Mortals endeavoured to probe its

Deep secrets. . . ."
But my people did not die as rebels;
They were not killed in the field
Of battle; nor did the earthquake
Shatter my country and subdue them.
Death was their only rescuer, and
Starvation their only spoils.

*   *   *   *   *

My people died on the cross. . . .
They died while their hands
Stretched toward the East and West,
While the remnants of their eyes
Stared at the blackness of the
Firmament. . . . They died silently,
For humanity had closed its ears
To their cry. They died because
They did not befriend their enemy.
They died because they loved their
Neighbours. They died because
They placed trust in all humanity.
They died because they did not
Oppress the oppressors. They died

Because they were the crushed
Flowers, and not the crushing feet.
They died because they were peace
Makers. They perished from hunger
In a land rich with milk and honey.
They died because the monsters of
Hell arose and destroyed all that
Their fields grew, and devoured the
Last provisions in their bins. . . .
They died because the vipers and
Sons of vipers spat out poison into
The space where the Holy Cedars and
The roses and the jasmine breathe
Their fragrance.

My people and your people, my Syrian
Brother, are dead. . . . What can be
Done for those who are dying? Our
Lamentations will not satisfy their
Hunger, and our tears will not quench
Their thirst; what can we do to save
Them from between the iron paws of
Hunger? My brother, the kindness

Which compels you to give a part of
Your life to any human who is in the
Shadow of losing his life is the only
Virtue which makes you worthy of the
Light of day and the peace of the
Night. . . . Remember, my brother,
That the coin which you drop into
The withered hand stretching toward
You is the only golden chain that
Binds your rich heart to the
Loving heart of God. . . .

The Ambitious Violet

The Ambitious Violet

THERE was a beautiful and fragrant violet who lived placidly amongst her friends, and swayed happily amidst the other flowers in a solitary garden. One morning, as her crown was embellished with beads of dew, she lifted her head and looked about; she saw a tall and handsome rose standing proudly and reaching high into space, like a burning torch upon an emerald lamp.

The violet opened her blue lips and said, "What an unfortunate am I among these flowers, and how humble is the position I occupy in their presence! Nature has fashioned me to be short and poor. . . . I live very close to the earth and I cannot raise my head toward the blue sky, or turn my face to the sun, as the roses do."

And the rose heard her neighbour's words; she laughed and commented, "How strange is your talk! You are fortunate, and yet you cannot understand your fortune. Nature has bestowed upon you fragrance and beauty which she did not grant to any other. . . . Cast aside your thoughts and be contented, and remember that he who humbles himself will be exalted, and he who exalts himself will be crushed."

The violet answered, "You are consoling me because you have that which I crave. . . . You seek to embitter me with the meaning that you are great. . . . How painful is the preaching of the fortunate to the heart of the miserable! And how severe is the strong when he stands as advisor among the weak!"

*   *   *   *   *

And Nature heard the conversation of the violet and the rose; she approached and said, "What has happened to you, my daughter violet? You have been humble and sweet in all your deeds and words. Has greed entered your heart and numbed your senses?" In a pleading voice, the violet answered her, saying, "Oh great and merciful mother, full of love and sympathy, I beg you, with all my heart and soul, to grant my request and allow me to be a rose for one day."

And Nature responded, "You know not what you are seeking; you are unaware of the concealed disaster behind your blind ambition. If you were a rose you would be sorry, and repentance would avail you but naught." The violet insisted, "Change me into a tall rose, for I wish to lift my head high with pride; and regardless of my fate, it will be my own doing." Nature yielded, saying, "Oh ignorant and rebellious violet, I will grant your request. But if calamity befalls you, your complaint must be to yourself."

And Nature stretched forth her mysterious and magic fingers and touched the roots of the violet, who immediately turned into a tall rose, rising above all other flowers in the garden.

At eventide the sky became thick with black clouds, and the raging elements disturbed the silence of existence with thunder, and commenced to attack the garden, sending forth a great rain and strong winds. The tempest tore the branches and uprooted the plants and broke the stems of the tall flowers, sparing only the little ones who grew close to the friendly earth. That solitary garden suffered greatly from the belligerent skies, and when the storm calmed and the sky cleared, all the flowers were laid waste and none of them had escaped the wrath of Nature except the clan of small violets, hiding by the wall of the garden.

*   *   *   *   *

Having lifted her head and viewed the tragedy of the flowers and trees, one of the violet maidens smiled happily and called to her companions, saying, "See what the tempest has done to the haughty flowers!" Another violet said, "We are small, and live close to the earth, but we are safe from the wrath of the skies." And a third one added, "Because we are poor in height the tempest is unable to subdue us."

At that moment the queen of violets saw by her side the converted violet, hurled to earth by the storm and distorted upon the wet grass like a limp soldier in a battle field. The queen of the violets lifted her head and called to her family, saying, "Look, my daughters, and meditate upon that which Greed has done to the violet who became a proud rose for one hour. Let the memory of this scene be a reminder of your good fortune."

And the dying rose moved and gathered the remnants of her strength, and quietly said, "You are contented and meek dullards; I have never feared the tempest. Yesterday I, too, was satisfied and contented with Life, but Contentment has acted as a barrier between my existence and the tempest of Life, confining me to a sickly and sluggish peace and tranquility of mind. I could have lived the same life you are living now by clinging with fear to the earth. . . . I could have waited for winter to shroud me with snow and deliver me to Death, who will surely claim all violets. . . . I am happy now because I have probed outside my little world into the mystery of the Universe . . . something which you have not yet done. I could have overlooked Greed, whose nature is higher than mine, but as I hearkened to the silence of the night, I heard the heavenly world talking to this earthly world, saying,

'Ambition beyond existence is the essential purpose of our being.' At that moment my spirit revolted and my heart longed for a position higher than my limited existence. I realized that the abyss cannot hear the song of the stars, and at that moment I commenced fighting against my smallness and craving for that which did not belong to me, until my rebelliousness turned into a great power, and my longing into a creating will. . . . Nature, who is the great object of our deeper dreams, granted my request and changed me into a rose with her magic fingers."

The rose became silent for a moment, and in a weakening voice, mingled with pride and achievement, she said, "I have lived one hour as a proud rose; I have existed for a time like a queen; I have looked at the Universe from behind the eyes of the rose; I have heard the whisper of the firmament through the ears of the rose and touched the folds of Light's garment with rose petals. Is there any here who can claim such honour?" Having thus spoken, she lowered her head, and with a choking voice she gasped, "I shall die now, for my soul has attained its goal. I have finally extended my knowledge to a world beyond the narrow cavern of my birth. This is the design of Life. . . . This is the secret of Existence." Then the rose quivered, slowly folded her petals, and breathed her last with a heavenly smile upon her lips . . . a smile of fulfillment of hope and purpose in Life . . . a smile of victory . . . a God's smile.

The Crucified

The Crucified

(*Written on Good Friday*)

Today, and on this same day of each year, man is startled from his deep slumber and stands before the phantoms of the Ages, looking with tearful eyes toward Mount Calvary to witness Jesus the Nazarene nailed on the Cross. . . . But when the day is over and eventide comes, human kinds return and kneel praying before the idols, erected upon every hilltop, every prairie, and every barter of wheat.

Today, the Christian souls ride on the wing of memories and fly to Jerusalem. There they will stand in throngs, beating upon their bosoms, and staring at Him, crowned with a wreath of thorns, stretching His arms before heaven, and looking from behind the veil of Death into the depths of Life. . . .

But when the curtain of night drops over the

stage of the day and the brief drama is concluded, the Christians will go back in groups and lie down in the shadow of oblivion between the quilts of ignorance and slothfulness.

On this one day of each year, the philosophers leave their dark caves, and the thinkers their cold cells, and the poets their imaginary arbors, and all stand reverently upon that silent mountain, listening to the voice of a young man saying of His killers, "Oh Father, forgive them, for they know not what they are doing."

But as dark silence chokes the voices of the light, the philosophers and the thinkers and the poets return to their narrow crevices and shroud their souls with meaningless pages of parchment.

The women who busy themselves in the splendour of Life will bestir themselves today from their cushions to see the sorrowful woman standing before the Cross like a tender sapling before the raging tempest; and when they approach near to her, they will hear a deep moaning and a painful grief.

The young men and women who are racing

with the torrent of modern civilization will halt today for a moment, and look backward to see the young Magdalen washing with her tears the blood stains from the feet of a Holy Man suspended between Heaven and Earth; and when their shallow eyes weary of the scene they will depart and soon laugh.

On this day of each year, Humanity wakes with the awakening of the Spring, and stands crying below the suffering Nazarene; then she closes her eyes and surrenders herself to a deep slumber. But Spring will remain awake, smiling and progressing until merged into Summer, dressed in scented golden raiment. Humanity is a mourner who enjoys lamenting the memories and heroes of the Ages. . . . If Humanity were possessed of understanding, there would be rejoicing over their glory. Humanity is like a child standing in glee by a wounded beast. Humanity laughs before the strengthening torrent which carries into oblivion the dry branches of the trees, and sweeps away with determination all things not fastened to strength.

Humanity looks upon Jesus the Nazarene as a poor-born Who suffered misery and humiliation with all of the weak. And He is pitied, for Humanity believes He was crucified painfully. . . . And all that Humanity offers to Him is crying and wailing and lamentation. For centuries Humanity has been worshipping weakness in the person of the Saviour.

The Nazarene was not weak! He was strong and is strong! But the people refuse to heed the true meaning of strength.

Jesus never lived a life of fear, nor did He die suffering or complaining. . . . He lived as a leader; He was crucified as a crusader; He died with a heroism that frightened His killers and tormentors.

Jesus was not a bird with broken wings; He was a raging tempest who broke all crooked wings. He feared not His persecutors nor His enemies. He suffered not before His killers. Free and brave and daring He was. He defied all despots and oppressors. He saw the contagious pustules and amputated them. . . . He muted Evil and He crushed Falsehood and He choked Treachery.

Jesus came not from the heart of the circle of Light to destroy the homes and build upon their ruins the convents and monasteries. He did not persuade the strong man to become a monk or a priest, but He came to send forth upon this earth a new spirit, with power to crumble the foundation of any monarchy built upon human bones and skulls. . . . He came to demolish the majestic palaces, constructed upon the graves of the weak, and crush the idols, erected upon the bodies of the poor. Jesus was not sent here to teach the people to build magnificent churches and temples amidst the cold wretched huts and dismal hovels. . . . He came to make the human heart a temple, and the soul an altar, and the mind a priest.

These were the missions of Jesus the Nazarene, and these are the teachings for which He was crucified. And if Humanity were wise, she would stand today and sing in strength the song of conquest and the hymn of triumph.

*   *   *   *   *

Oh, Crucified Jesus, Who art looking sorrow-fully from Mount Calvary at the sad procession of the Ages, and hearing the clamour of the dark nations, and understanding the dreams of Eternity . . . Thou art, on the Cross, more glorious and dignified than one thousand kings upon one thousand thrones in one thousand empires. . . . .

Thou art, in the agony of death, more power-ful than one thousand generals in one thousand wars. . . .

With Thy sorrows, Thou art more joyous than Spring with its flowers. . . .

With Thy suffering, Thou art more bravely silent than the crying angels of heaven. . . .

Before Thy lashers, Thou art more resolute than the mountain of rock. . . .

Thy wreath of thorns is more brilliant and sub-lime than the crown of Bahram. . . . The nails piercing Thy hands are more beautiful than the sceptre of Jupiter. . . .

The spatters of blood upon Thy feet are more resplendent than the necklace of Ishtar.

Forgive the weak who lament Thee today, for

they do not know how to lament themselves. . . .

Forgive them, for they do not know that Thou
hast conquered death with death, and bestowed
life upon the dead. . . .

Forgive them, for they do not know that Thy
strength still awaits them. . . .

Forgive them, for they do not know that every
day is Thy day.

Eventide of the Feast

Eventide of the Feast

NIGHT HAD FALLEN and obscurity engulfed the city while the lights glittered in the palaces and the huts and the shops. The multitudes, wearing their festive raiment, crowded the streets and upon their faces appeared the signs of celebration and contentment.

I avoided the clamour of the throngs and walked alone, contemplating the Man Whose greatness they were honouring, and meditating the Genius of the Ages Who was born in poverty, and lived virtuously, and died on the Cross.

I was pondering the burning torch which was lighted in this humble village in Syria by the Holy Spirit. . . . The Holy Spirit Who hovers over all the ages, and penetrates one civilization and then another through His truth.

As I reached the public garden, I seated myself on a rustic bench and commenced looking between the naked trees toward the crowded streets; I listened to the hymns and songs of the celebrants.

After an hour of deep thinking, I looked sidewise and was surprised to find a man sitting by me, holding a short branch with which he engraved vague figures on the ground. I was startled, for I had not seen nor heard his approach, but I said within myself, "He is solitary, as I am." And after looking thoroughly at him, I saw that in spite of his old-fashioned raiment and long hair, he was a dignified man, worthy of attention. It seemed that he detected the thoughts within me, for in a deep and quiet voice he said, "Good evening, my son."

"Good evening to you," I responded with respect.

And he resumed his drawing while the strangely soothing sound of his voice was still echoing in my ears. And I spoke to him again, saying, "Are you a stranger in this city?"

"Yes, I am a stranger in this city and every city," he replied. I consoled him, adding, "A stranger should forget that he is an outsider in these holidays, for there is kindness and generosity in the people." He replied wearily, "I am more a stranger in these days than in any other." Having thus spoken, he looked at the clear skies; his eyes probed the stars and his lips quivered as if he had found in the firmament an image of a distant country. His queer statement aroused my interest, and I said, "This is the time of the year when the people are kind to all other people. The rich remember the poor and the strong have compassion for the weak."

He returned, "Yes, the momentary mercy of the rich upon the poor is bitter, and the sympathy of the strong toward the weak is naught but a reminder of superiority."

I affirmed, "Your.words have merit, but the weak poor do not care to know what transpires in the heart of the rich, and the hungry never think of the method by which the bread he is craving is kneaded and baked."

And he responded, "The one who receives is not mindful, but the one who gives bears the burden of cautioning himself that it is with a view to brotherly love, and toward friendly aid, and not to self-esteem."

I was amazed at his wisdom, and again commenced to meditate upon his ancient appearance and strange garments. Then I returned mentally and said, "It appears that you are in need of help; will you accept a few coins from me?" And with a sad smile he answered me, saying, "Yes, I am in desperate need, but not of gold or silver."

Puzzled, I asked, "What is it that you require?"

"I am in need of shelter. I am in need of a place where I ran rest my head and my thoughts."

"Please accept these two denars and go to the inn for lodging," I insisted.

Sorrowfully he answered, "I have tried every inn, and knocked at every door, but in vain. I have entered every food shop, but none cared to help me. I am hurt, not hungry; I am disappointed, not tired; I seek not a roof, but human shelter."

I said within myself, "What a strange person he is! Once he talks like a philosopher and again like a madman!" As I whispered these thoughts into the ears of my inner self, he stared at me, lowered his voice to a sad level, and said, "Yes, I am a madman, but even a madman will find himself a stranger without shelter and hungry without food, for the heart of man is empty."

I apologized to him, saying, "I regret my unwitting thought. Would you accept my hospitality and take shelter in my quarters?"

"I knocked at your door and all the doors one thousand times, and received no answer," he answered severely.

Now I was convinced that he was truly a madman, and I suggested, "Let us go now, and proceed to my home."

He lifted his head slowly and said, "If you were aware of my identity you would not invite me to your home."

"Who are you?" I inquired, fearfully, slowly.

With a voice that sounded like the roar of the ocean, he thundered, bitterly, "I am the revolution who builds what the nations destroy. . . . I am the tempest who uproots the plants, grown by the ages. . . . I am the one who came to spread war on earth and not peace, for man is content only in misery!"

And, with tears coursing down his cheeks, he stood up high, and a mist of light grew about him, and he stretched forth his arms, and I saw the marks of the nails in the palms of his hands; I prostrated myself before him convulsively and cried out, saying, "Oh Jesus, the Nazarene!"

And He continued, in anguish, "The people are celebrating in My honour, pursuing the tradition woven by the ages around My name, but as to Myself, I am a stranger wandering from East to West upon this earth, and no one knows of Me. The foxes have their holes, and the birds of the skies their nests, but the Son of Man has no place to rest His head."

At that moment, I opened my eyes, lifted my head, and looked around, but found naught except a column of smoke before me, and I heard only the shivering voice of the silence of the night, coming from the depths of Eternity. I collected myself and looked again to the singing throngs in the distance, and a voice within me said, "The very strength that protects the heart from injury is the strength that prevents the heart from enlarging to its intended greatness within. The song of the voice is sweet, but the song of the heart is the pure voice of heaven."

The Grave Digger

The Grave Digger

In the terrible silence of the night, as all heavenly things disappeared behind the grasping veil of thick clouds, I walked lonely and afraid in the Valley of the Phantoms of Death.

As midnight came, and the spectres leaped about me with their horrible, ribbed wings, I observed a giant ghost standing before me, fascinating me with his hypnotic ghastliness. In a thundering voice he said, "Your fear is two-fold! You fear being in fear of me! You cannot conceal it, for you are weaker than the thin thread of the spider. What is your earthly name?"

I leaned against a great rock, gathered myself from this sudden shock, and in a sickly, trembling voice replied, "My name is Abdallah, which means 'slave of God.'" For a few moments he remained silent with a frightening silence. I grew accustomed to his appearance, but was again shaken by his weird thoughts and words, his strange beliefs and contemplations.

He rumbled, "Numerous are the slaves of God, and great are God's woes with His slaves. Why did not your father call you 'Master of Demons' instead, adding one more disaster to the huge calamity of earth? You cling with terror to the small circle of gifts from your ancestors, and your affliction is caused by your parents' bequest, and you will remain a slave of death until you become one of the dead.

"Your vocations are wasteful and deserted, and your lives are hollow. Real life has never visited you, nor will it; neither will your deceitful self realize your living death. Your illusioned eyes see the people quivering before the tempest of life and you believe them to be alive, while in truth they have been dead since they were born. There were none who would bury them, and the one good career for you is that of grave digger, and as such you may rid the few living of the corpses heaped about the homes, the paths, and the churches."

I protested, "I cannot pursue such a vocation.

My wife and children require my support and companionship."

He leaned toward me, showing his braided muscles that seemed as the roots of a strong oak tree, abounding with life and energy, and he bellowed, "Give to each a spade and teach them to dig graves; your life is naught but black misery hidden behind walls of white plaster. Join us, for we genii are the only possessors of reality! The digging of graves brings a slow but positive benefit which causes the vanishing of the dead creatures who tremble with the storm and never walk with it." He mused and then inquired, "What is your religion?"

Bravely I stated, "I believe in God and I honour His prophets; I love virtue and I have faith in eternity."

With remarkable wisdom and conviction he responded, "These empty words were placed on human lips by past ages and not by knowledge, and you actually believe in yourself only; and you honour none but yourself, and you have faith only in the eternity of your desires. Man has worshipped his own self since the beginning, calling that self by appropriate titles, until now, when he employs the word 'God' to mean that same self." Then the giant roared with laughter, the echoes reverberating through the hollows of the caverns, and he taunted, "How strange are those who worship their own selves, their real existence being naught but earthly carcasses!"

He paused, and I contemplated his sayings and meditated their meanings. He possessed a knowledge stranger than life and more terrible than death, and deeper than truth. Timidly, I ventured, "Do you have a religion or a God?"

"My name is The Mad God," he offered, "and I was born at all times, and I am the god of my own self. I am not wise, for wisdom is a quality of the weak. I am strong, and the earth moves under the steps of my feet, and when I stop, the procession of stars stops with me. I mock at the people. . . . I accompany the giants of night. . . . I mingle with the great kings of the genii. . . . I am in possession of the secrets of existence and non-existence.

"In the morning I blaspheme the sun . . . at noontide I curse humanity . . . at eventide I submerge nature . . . at night I kneel and worship myself. I never sleep, for I am time, the sea, and myself. . . . I eat human bodies for food, drink their blood to quench my thirst, and use their dying gasps to draw my breath. Although you deceive yourself, you are my brother and you live as I do. Begone . . . hypocrite! Crawl back to earth and continue to worship your own self amid the living dead!"

I staggered from the rocky, cavernous valley in narcotic bewilderment, scarcely believing what my ears had heard and my eyes had seen! I was torn in pain by some of the truths he had spoken, and wandered through the fields all that night in melancholy contemplation.

*   *   *   *   *

I procured a spade and said within myself, "Dig deeply the graves. . . . Go, now, and wherever you find one of the living dead, bury him in the earth."

Since that day I have been digging graves and burying the living dead. But the living dead are numerous and I am alone, having none to aid me. . . .

Honeyed Poison

Honeyed Poison

İᴛ ᴡᴀs a beautiful morn of dizzying brilliance in North Lebanon when the people of the village of Tula gathered around the portico of the small church that stood in the midst of their dwellings. They were discussing busily the sudden and unexplained departure of Farris Rahal, who left behind his bride of but half a year.

Farris Rahal was the Sheik and leader of the village, and he had inherited this honourable status from his ancestors who had ruled over Tula for centuries. Although he was not quite twenty-seven years of age, he possessed an outstanding ability and sincerity that won the admiration, reverence, and respect of all the fellahin. When Farris married Susan, the people commented upon him, saying, "What a fortunate man is Farris Rahal! He has attained all that man can hope for in the bounty of life's happiness, and he is but a youth!"

That morning, when all of Tula arose from slumber and learned that the Sheik had gathered his gold, mounted his steed and left the village bidding none farewell, curiosity and concern prevailed, and inquiries were many as to the cause that prompted him to desert his wife and his home, his lands and his vineyards.

*   *   *   *   *

By reason of tradition and geography, life in North Lebanon is highly sociable, and the people share their joys and sorrows, provoked by humble spirit and instinctive clannishness. Upon any occurrence, the entire populace of the village convenes to inquire upon the incident, offers all possible assistance, and returns to labour until fate again offers a congregant mission.

It was such a matter that drew the people of Tula from their work that day, and caused them to gather about the church of Mar Tula discussing the departure of their Sheik and exchanging views upon its singularity.

It was at this time that Father Estephan, head of the local church, arrived, and upon his drawn countenance one could read the unmistakable signs of deep suffering, the signs of a painfully wounded spirit. He contemplated the scene for a moment and then spoke. "Do not ask . . . do not ask any question of me! Before daybreak this day, Sheik Farris knocked upon the door of my house, and I saw him holding the rein of his horse, and from his face emanated grave sorrow and agonized grief. Upon my remark as to the strangeness of the hour, he replied, 'Father, I come to bid you farewell, for I am sailing beyond the oceans and will never again return to this land.' And he handed to me a sealed envelope, addressed to his dearest friend Nabih Malik, asking me to deliver it. He mounted his steed and sped off to the east, affording me no further opportunity to understand the purpose of his unusual departure."

One of the villagers observed, "Undoubtedly the missive will reveal to us the secret of his going, for Nabih is his closest friend." Another added, "Have you seen his bride, Father?" The priest replied, saying, "I visited her after the morning prayer and found her standing at the window, staring with unseeing eyes at something invisible, appearing as one who has lost all senses, and when I endeavoured to ask concerning Farris she merely said, 'I do not know! I do not know!' Then she wept like a child who suddenly becomes an orphan."

As the father concluded talking, the group tightened with fear at the startling report of a gunshot coming from the east portion of the village, and it was followed immediately by the bitter wailing of a woman. The throng was in a dismayed trance of immobility for a moment, and then, men, women and children, all ran toward the scene, and upon their faces there was a dark mask of fear and evil omen. As they reached the garden that surrounded the Sheik's residence, they became witness to a most horrible drama, portrayed with death. Nabih Malik was lying on the ground, a stream of blood issuing from his breast, and by him stood Susan, wife of the Sheik Farris Rahal, tearing her hair and shredding her raiment and flailing her arms about and shrieking wildly, "Nabih . . . Nabih . . . why did you do it!"

The onlookers were astounded, and it was as though the unseen hands of fate had clutched with icy fingers at their hearts. The priest found in the dead Nabih's right hand the note he had delivered that morning, and he placed it deftly into his robe without notice by the milling multitude.

Nabih was carried to his miserable mother, who, upon seeing the lifeless body of her only son, lost her sanity in shock and soon joined him in Eternity. Susan was led slowly into her home, wavering between faltering life and grasping death.

As Father Estephan reached his home, under bent shoulders, he fastened the door, adjusted his reading glasses, and in a quivering whisper commenced reading to himself the message he had taken from the hand of the departed Nabih.

"My Dearest Friend Nabih,

"I must leave this village of my fathers, for my continued presence is casting misery upon you and upon my wife and upon myself. You are noble in spirit, and scorn the betrayal of friend or neighbour, and although I know that Susan is innocent and virtuous, I know also that the true love which unites your heart and her heart is beyond your power and beyond my hopes. I cannot struggle longer against the mighty will of God, as I cannot halt the strong flow of the great Kadeesha River.

"You have been my sincere friend, Nabih, since we played as children in the fields; and before God, believe me, you remain my friend. I beg you to ponder with good thoughts upon me in the future as you did in the past. Tell Susan that I love her and that I wronged her by taking her in empty marriage. Tell her that my heart bled in burning pain each time I turned from restless sleep in the silence of the night and observed her kneeling before the shrine of Jesus, weeping and beating upon her bosom in anguish.

"There is no punishment so severe as that suffered by the woman who finds herself imprisoned between a man she loves and another man who loves her. Susan suffered through a constant and painful conflict, but performed sorrowfully and honourably and silently her duties as a wife. She tried, but could not choke her honest love for you.

"I am leaving for distant lands and will never again return, for I can no longer act as barrier to a genuine and eternal love, embraced by the enfolded arms of God; and may God, in his inscrutable wisdom, protect and bless both of you.

"FARRIS"

Father Estephan folded the letter, returned it to his pocket, and sat by the window that opened upon the distant valley. He sailed long and deep in a great ocean of contemplation, and after wise and intense meditation, he stood suddenly, as if he had found between the plaited folds of his intricate thoughts a delicate and horrible secret, disguised with diabolical slyness, and wrapped with elaborate cunning! He cried out, "How sagacious you are, Farris! How massive, yet simple, is your crime! You sent to him honey blended with fatal poison, and enclosed death in a letter! And when Nabih pointed the weapon at his heart, it was your finger that discharged the missile, and it was your will that engulfed his will. . . . How clever you are, Farris!"

He returned quivering to his chair, shaking his head and combing his beard with his fingers, and upon his lips appeared a smile whose meaning was more terrible than the tragedy itself. He opened his prayer book and commenced reading and pondering, and at intervals he raised his head to hear the wailing and lamentations of the women, coming from the heart of the village of Tula, close by the Holy Cedars of Lebanon.